Cold Email Success in 24 Hours

From Prospects to Profits

JOHN LEWIS

DISCLAIMER!

The contents of the book **"Cold Email Success in 24 Hours,"** including, but not limited to, the text, graphics, images, and other material contained within, are the exclusive property of the author and are protected under international copyright laws.

Table of Contents

INTRODUCTION

C old emailing has become a powerful tool for businesses and professionals seeking to connect with potential clients, partners, and opportunities. Unlike traditional marketing methods, cold emailing offers a direct and personal way to reach out to individuals who may benefit from your products, services, or insights. However, the success of cold emailing hinges on a delicate balance of strategy, personalization, and persistence. This book, "Cold Emailing Strategies: A Comprehensive Guide," aims to demystify the art and science of cold emailing, providing you with the knowledge and tools needed to craft compelling messages, build meaningful relationships, and achieve your goals.

Cold emails have several distinct advantages, contributing to their power in modern business. First, they are cost-effective. Unlike expensive advertising campaigns or direct mail, sending an email incurs minimal costs, making it an attractive option for businesses of all sizes, especially startups and small enterprises with limited marketing budgets. This cost-effectiveness allows for a higher return on investment, particularly when emails are well-crafted and strategically targeted.

Second, cold emails offer scalability. With the right tools and strategies, businesses can send personalized emails to many recipients without significant additional effort. This scalability is invaluable for companies looking to expand their reach quickly and efficiently. Furthermore, cold emails can be automated, enabling businesses to maintain consistent communication with their prospects and follow up systematically.

Another critical aspect of cold emails is their ability to bypass traditional gatekeepers. In many industries, reaching key decision-makers through conventional means can be challenging because of layers of intermediaries. Cold emails provide a direct line of communication, increasing the likelihood of your message being seen by the right person. This directness saves time and enhances the chances of starting a meaningful conversation that can lead to business opportunities.

Personalization is where cold emails truly shine. A well-crafted cold email can address the recipient's specific needs and interests, making it far more likely to resonate and elicit a positive response. Personalization goes beyond merely inserting the recipient's Name; it involves tailoring the content to align with their business objectives, pain points, and recent achievements. This level of customization demonstrates that you have done your homework and genuinely understand their business, fostering trust and engagement.

Moreover, cold emails provide measurable results. Unlike some traditional marketing methods, cold emailing allows for detailed tracking and analysis. Businesses can monitor open rates, click-through rates, and response rates to assess the effectiveness of their campaigns. This data-driven approach enables continuous improvement, allowing businesses to refine their strategies based on what works best for their audience.

Throughout this guide, we will explore the fundamental principles of cold emailing, from understanding its significance in modern business to mastering the nuances of crafting effective emails. You will learn how to build a targeted email list, write attention-grabbing subject lines, and create persuasive content that resonates with your audience. We will delve into the importance of personalization and segmentation, offering techniques to tailor your emails for maximum impact. Additionally, we will cover the best practices for timing and frequency, ensuring your emails are sent at the optimal moments to capture your recipients' attention.

The journey does not end with sending the initial email. Follow-up strategies play a crucial role in converting potential leads into valuable connections. This book will guide you through the process of effective follow-ups, helping you stay persistent without being intrusive. Moreover, you will gain insights into analyzing and optimizing your email campaigns, using data-driven methods to measure success and improve continuously.

By the end of this book, you will be equipped with advanced cold emailing techniques, real-world case studies, and a glimpse into the future trends of this dynamic field. Whether you are a seasoned marketer looking to refine your skills or a newcomer eager to make your mark, "Cold Emailing Strategies: A Comprehensive Guide" will be your essential companion on the path to the success of cold emailing. Let's embark on this journey together and unlock the potential of cold emailing to transform your professional endeavors.

WHAT IS COLD EMAILING?

A well-known Harvard Business School professor reportedly asked his students to identify the most common reason for business failure. He received various responses, ranging from inadequate management and programs to subpar products, weak conceptions, and a lack of funds. After reviewing their responses, he stated that the primary reason for business failure was "lack of sales."

That is it. It's a lack of genuine sales—the work you and I perform on the front lines. And if I can't get in the door to see folks, I won't sell. In most sales environments, nothing can happen until you get that first appointment. No matter how good you sell, if you can't get through the door or obtain an appointment to see someone, you won't sell.

To succeed as a salesperson, you must build a strong prospect base. This foundation will only be solidified if you continue to prospect successfully — and cold calling is an important part of that process. Cold calling is the best and most cost-effective technique to develop prospects continuously.

Therefore, cold emailing is a strategic method of reaching out to potential clients, partners, or stakeholders who have not previously interacted with or shown interest in the sender's products or services. The primary purpose of cold emailing is to initiate a professional relationship and generate interest, whether it be for sales, networking, collaboration, or other business opportunities.

Unlike warm emailing, which targets individuals who have already expressed some level of interest, cold emailing involves contacting recipients who may be unaware of the sender or their offerings. Effective cold emailing requires careful planning, personalization, and a clear value proposition to capture the recipient's attention and encourage a positive response.

Effective cold emails are personalized, relevant, and crafted to grab the recipient's attention and encourage a positive response. They are a vital tool in modern business for reaching out to potential clients, partners, or collaborators who may not be aware of the sender's offerings.

Hence, do you know your number one competitor? Interestingly, you can name every company in your business and be wrong. I will inform you that you are incorrect, regardless of the firm you mentioned. You may tell me you're your own competitor. You'd be wrong again. You could say that your energy level is your competition. Wrong.

Today's number one competitor is the status quo. People are currently maintaining the status quo. If you grasp this, you'll be successful. We rarely face competition; instead, we typically face the incumbent or the status quo. Remember that most potential consumers are satisfied with what they have — otherwise, they would contact you!

When conducting a training session, I mentioned that your number one competition is the status quo. A sales representative raised his hand and stated, "Steve, I have never heard of that company. "Who is Status Quo?" Do not get diverted. Remember that you're competing with how your prospects are currently conducting business!

Where Sales Come From

First, I'd like to tackle an issue many salespeople are upset about. The truth is that regardless of what you do, you will receive one-third of all your sales. Let me repeat: regardless of what you do, you will receive one-third of all sales.

In the United States, almost 1,000 copiers are sold every hour of every day. About 2,000 cellphone numbers are estimated to be activated in the United States each hour.

What do figures like those tell you about sales? They should emphasize the need for your goods, similar to how you would need to buy milk at the supermarket. That is a customer-driven sale.

In fact, you and I have witnessed persons who should not be permitted to walk the streets without a leash making transactions. People like that may make a living because their sales are based on consumer demand for those things.

Something will break eventually; you will need a new car, extra vegetables, and a television. Successful salespeople recognize that they will get one-third of their sales anyway because they knock on enough doors. But is this enough?

The Sales You Will Never Get

Then there's one-third of your sales that you won't receive. For some reason, no matter what you do, you will not receive the remaining one-third of your sales. Sometimes, it's because the other guy, the other salesperson, understands it. You cannot always control internal changes at the target company. In either case, you won't receive the business.

Sales Opportunities

The final one-third is up for grabs. That is what we will explore here. We'll show you how to get a competitive advantage, book more appointments, and increase your share of the last one-third, which is where good salespeople differentiate themselves from average salespeople.

Intriguingly, many salespeople make their income by only accepting the first one-third. That's more of an order-taking scenario.

In fact, a person in Times Square sells a small wallet-style card case. He merely stands there and repeats, "Wanna buy, wanna buy, wanna buy, wanna buy, wanna buy, wanna buy?" You get the idea. That is all he does!

That reveals something about the overall sales process. If you meet enough individuals, you will ultimately make a sale. In fact, as previously said, you will make a fixed number of sales regardless of what you do. If you knock on enough doors, it doesn't matter what you do; you'll ultimately get a sale.

Assume someone stood on the busiest street corner near an office, such as Times Square, and just extended their hand. Someone might eventually hand them money. Now, if they included a cup, they might make more money. Adding a cup and a bell, bing-bing-bing-bing is likely to increase the number of individuals who donate money. Adding a cup, a bell, bing-bing-bing-bing, and a sign reading "Please help me" would boost contributions even more.

This example demonstrates that, while making a sale is achievable with enough attempts, it is also critical to maximize the opportunity. Simply seeing or talking to individuals on the phone is insufficient; employing the appropriate tools is required.

In Manhattan, beside an office, a bank had a table with the sign "SIGN UP FOR PC BANKING." Three bank staff approached each passerby. When asked how they did it, they replied that they had signed up 200 customers for their PC banking software in just two hours. Similarly, a big telecoms provider began years ago by putting up tables outside prominent office buildings with the words "SAVE MONEY ON LONG DISTANCE," and customers would sign up. Building a great sales career requires more than just one attempt.

Timing is everything. Examining the prospecting process demonstrates the value of time. It usually takes around eight weeks from the first meeting with a prospective client to closing the deal. For example, if a conference occurs on January 1st, the sale is expected to close around March 1st. If the sales cycle lasts 18 weeks, the deadline is extended. Delays in prospecting push the estimated sale date back appropriately. If no prospecting occurs for several days in January, the sale date is delayed accordingly.

When considering whether a sale is profitable, it becomes clear that income today is the product of months or even years of prospecting. Today's Appointments generate prospects, which lead to sales after the sales cycle.

Reducing the Sales Cycle

On a recent sales call, scheduling a follow-up appointment during the first visit, rather than waiting, saved three to five weeks in the sales process. Typically, a salesperson will promise to call the prospect within a week, which adds at least one week to the cycle. Delays in reaching the prospect can push the schedule even further. This wasted time is eliminated by scheduling the following appointment during the original meeting, resulting in a sales cycle that is several weeks shorter.

Do the Numbers

When a friend's company was founded in 1980, there was no clear strategy for securing appointments. The expectation was that clients would initiate contact, leading to hiring a secretary and an associate to manage incoming calls. Despite having a well-defined product and a perceived demand for it, the belief was that sending out announcements would suffice to attract customers.

This approach proved ineffective, as demonstrated by the 10,000 unused brochures and pens still in possession.

The realization quickly set in that securing appointments was critical to success. It became evident that 65% of success in sales hinges on actively finding people and communicating what the business offers.

The A=P=S Formula

The most important formula for effective salespeople is A=P=S. In other words, appointments lead to prospects and then sales. What are your chances of acquiring a new prospect if you do not have any new appointments today? It is nonexistent. What are your chances of making a sale if you don't have any fresh prospects? That, too, is nonexistent. The fundamental question is, how many appointments are required to develop one real prospect? (A prospect is someone who has actively agreed to go through the sales process with you.

Understanding the relationship between appointments, prospects, and sales is essential. The number of appointments required to generate one real prospect, someone who agrees to proceed through the sales process, is crucial. The appointment base will always be larger than the prospect base, which in turn is larger than the sales base, resembling a pyramid structure with appointments at the base, prospects in the middle, and sales at the top.

For instance, not making any new appointments today means no new prospects will be generated, leading to no new sales approximately eight weeks later. The notion that clients will call on their own accounts for consumer-driven sales is distinct from the proactive approach needed to capture the remaining third of all potential sales. A=P=S, or simply put, zero appointments equals zero prospects equals zero sales.

Know Your Numbers

Understanding your key metrics is crucial for evaluating the effectiveness of your sales approach. Knowing how many appointments you need to secure prospects and how many calls it takes to achieve those appointments is essential. Without this knowledge, assessing the success of your sales strategy becomes challenging.

For example, achieving one appointment per day or five new appointments per week might require emailing 15 people daily. Over five days, this amounts to 75 emails, which can generate five new appointments, ultimately resulting in one sale per week. This illustrates the importance of knowing your numbers to reach your goals.

Consider how many cold calls you make each day. Are these calls to new prospects or repeats to the same individuals? Consistently reaching out to 15 new people daily can be disciplined, even on busy days. If contact during normal business hours is difficult, consider calling earlier in the morning. While early calls might not reach many people directly, leaving 15 messages can still yield responses.

Emailing 7 out of 15 contacts daily might result in one new appointment. Repeating this process five days a week can lead to five new appointments, with additional follow-up meetings scheduled subsequently. For every five new appointments, it is common to have three follow-through appointments, totaling eight appointments per week. With a closing ratio of one sale per eight appointments, this method could generate approximately 50 new accounts annually.

This approach emphasizes the importance of making consistent calls. Reducing the number of daily calls could adversely affect overall sales performance. Cold calling operates as a numbers game, where specific ratios drive success.

Reflect on your daily mail volume. Is it yielding the necessary number of appointments for success? For instance, achieving five new appointments weekly might require a certain number of daily emails and conversations. Understanding these numbers and how they are determined is vital.

Most people know their car's mileage but may not track the number of appointments they had the previous week. Knowing these figures is critical for achieving sales targets. Understanding and tracking your ratios can significantly impact your yearly income. Consistent sales growth can be achieved by securing even one additional appointment per day.

Many salespeople operate without a clear understanding of their key metrics. However, taking control of your career involves using numbers that reflect the actual sales and appointments needed daily, weekly, monthly, and annually.

Numbers from the Real World

Some significant numbers are 293 > 149 > 49 > 83 > 10. These are actual sales figures. In this case, a salesperson sent 293 emails over a 10-week period, spoke to 149 people, and set up 49 first appointments. The number 83 represents the total number of sales visits, which includes repeat or follow-through visits. Finally, 10 represents the number of sales. Analyzing these numbers reveals that the salesperson made one sale and attended an average of 8.3 weekly appointments for 10 weeks. This individual set up about five appointments every week and made approximately 30 emails a week, or six calls a day, for 10 weeks. Although these numbers are not exceptionally high, they demonstrate a successful strategy because the salesperson understood and monitored their metrics, achieving the goal of one new sale per week.

Another example involves an individual who made $68,000 in a year (in 1987 dollars) by making 2,448 phone calls. This averages out to 10 calls a day over a 250-day working year. This demonstrates that consistent effort, such as making 10 calls a day, can lead to substantial financial success. Each call brings the salesperson closer to a yes, illustrating the importance of persistence in sales.

Avoiding Peaks and Valleys

Prospecting and setting appointments are crucial for avoiding the peaks and valleys that many salespeople experience. These fluctuations are often unnecessary and result from consistently failing to replenish the prospect base. Considering the ratios previously discussed, each sale reduces the number of prospects. For example, if a salesperson starts with 20 prospects and has a closing ratio of one out of five, making a sale means four prospects have said no. This reduces the active prospect pool, and without replenishment, it continues to shrink with each sale.

Salespeople often cycle through their prospect lists without adding new prospects, creating highs and lows in their sales performance. It is essential to continuously replenish the prospect base to avoid these peaks and valleys. Depending on the sales cycle, this replenishment process can take weeks, months, or even longer. Regularly checking and replenishing the prospect base ensures a steady flow of potential sales, preventing the downturns that occur when the prospect pool is depleted.

Sales performance should be evaluated over extended periods to get an accurate picture. For example, a salesperson might have an exceptional month followed by a poor one, indicating the need for consistent prospecting efforts. By averaging sales over several months, salespeople can better understand their performance and maintain a steady stream of prospects to avoid the highs and lows commonly experienced in sales.

Prospecting and the Sales Cycle

The need for perpetual sales prospecting becomes evident when considering how far sales efforts occur in advance of sales revenues. For instance, if it takes 60 days to generate a sale, 30 days to implement the program, 30 days to use the service, 30 days to bill, and 30 days to get paid, six months pass between the start of the process and the actual receipt of revenue. The sales made today result from efforts made previously. Appointments = Prospects = Sales.

An illustrative case involved a software company that experienced a tremendous year. The president of the company noted that from January to June, they secured 15 major accounts from 15 inquiries, resulting in a successful period. However, inquiries stopped after that, leading to a significant downturn in sales. Their sales cycle, taking nearly a year, means they are now in danger of going under due to the lack of continuous prospecting.

Keep on Prospecting!

Even during successful periods, continuous prospecting is essential. A common mistake is to become complacent with existing business, neglecting the need to seek new prospects. Prospecting should be a daily activity to maintain a steady sales pipeline.

The importance of prospecting was highlighted when a busy period caused a temporary halt in prospecting efforts. Two months later, this led to a significant drop in sales, demonstrating the critical need for ongoing prospecting activities. Additionally, when a key salesperson fell ill, the lack of scheduled appointments during their absence underscored the necessity of maintaining regular prospecting efforts, even in challenging circumstances.

Managing prospects is crucial for sustaining sales. Without enough appointments, there won't be enough prospects, leading to insufficient sales and potential business failure. Regular prospecting helps avoid fluctuations in sales performance and ensures a steady flow of business opportunities. By keeping this concept in mind and consistently acting on it, businesses can maintain stability and growth. Appointments = Prospects = Sales.

The Value of a "No"

Understanding the value of a "no" is crucial in the context of cold emailing and sales. It's important to know how many appointments are needed each week and how many calls are required each day to achieve that number of appointments. Without these metrics, success is unlikely.

Receiving numerous "no" answers is an inevitable part of the process. Surprisingly, the number of "no" responses should not be a major concern. If "no" isn't heard frequently, it means that sales are not being made. This addresses the criticism that cold calling doesn't work all the time. It's not designed to be foolproof; instead, it provides a competitive edge by improving the current numbers.

There is a typical ratio of "no" answers to "yes" answers in cold calling. For example, making 20 calls might result in speaking to five people and setting up one appointment. Similarly, seeing 20 people might lead to five presentations and one sale. This means hearing "no" 19 times before getting one appointment or sale. Therefore, every "no" brings one closer to a "yes."

Life insurance companies and HMOs often use this approach. New life insurance agents are given a chart with 250 boxes to mark an X for each "no" answer they receive. When the chart is full, they receive $1,000. This is feasible because generating 250 "no" answers typically results in $10,000 in sales, making it profitable to pay for each "no."

Understanding this concept helps predict sales outcomes. By knowing the ratios, it's possible to estimate the time needed to reach a certain level of sales. For example, a new representative in Chicago was initially unsuccessful. By identifying the number of "no" responses required, it was determined that he needed just two more "no" answers to make a sale. Following this advice, he closed his first sale on his 101st day with the company.

In summary, tracking "no" answers is essential for sales success. Each "no" is a step closer to a "yes," making it a valuable part of the sales process.

Five Ways to Double Your Income

Consider these examples of call metrics to understand what to expect.

One sales force in New York made 606 calls, spoke to 315 people, and set up 152 appointments. Another salesperson in Chicago selling advertising made 736 calls, spoke to 358 people, and set up 138 appointments. In Los Angeles, a company made 203 calls, spoke to 99 people, and set up 66 new appointments. Similarly, a company in Florida made 589 calls, spoke to 213 people, and set up 102 appointments. These numbers demonstrate the effectiveness of this approach across different regions.

There are five ways to double income based on these numbers:

Five Ways to Double Your Income Through Cold Emailing

Doubling your income through cold emailing requires strategic enhancements in various aspects of your emailing process. Here are five detailed ways to achieve this:

1. Double the Number of Emails Sent

- **Email List Expansion**: Continuously grow your email list by leveraging multiple sources such as social media, networking events, online directories, and industry-specific databases. Use tools like Hunter.io or LinkedIn Sales Navigator to find and verify new email addresses.

- **Email Automation**: Implement email automation tools like Mailchimp, Sendinblue, or HubSpot to efficiently manage and send a large volume of emails. Automation helps you scale your efforts without compromising personalization.

- **Template Library**: Develop a library of customizable email templates for different sales funnel stages. This saves time and ensures consistency in your messaging, allowing you to send more emails with less effort.

2. Improve Open Rates

- **Compelling Subject Lines**: Craft subject lines that are attention-grabbing and relevant to the recipient. Personalize them with the recipient's Name or mention a specific interest or pain point. A/B tests different subject lines to determine which ones yield the highest open rates.

- **Preheader Text**: Utilize the preheader text to provide a sneak peek of your email content. This text should complement your subject line and entice the recipient to open the email.

- **Optimize Send Times**: Research and experiment to find the best times to send your emails. Generally, mid-week and mid-morning are effective times, but adjust based on your target audience's habits.

3. Increase Response Rates

- **Engaging Content**: Ensure your email content is concise, relevant, and engaging. Address the recipient's specific needs or challenges and offer a clear solution. Use bullet points, short paragraphs, and clear headers to make the content easily scannable.

- **Strong Call to Action (CTA)**: Include a clear and compelling CTA. Whether it's scheduling a call, signing up for a demo, or downloading a resource, make sure it's easy for the recipient to take the next step.

- **Follow-Up Strategy**: Develop a robust follow-up strategy. Send polite, persistent follow-up emails if you don't get a response to your initial email. Use tools that automate follow-ups while maintaining personalization.

4. Convert More Appointments to Sales

- **Preparation**: Before the appointment, research the prospect thoroughly. Understand their business, industry challenges, and potential needs. Tailor your pitch to address these specific aspects.

- **Value Presentation**: Focus on presenting the value of your product or service rather than just its features. Use case studies, testimonials, and data to demonstrate how your solution can solve their problems or improve their operations.

- **Address Objections**: Be prepared to address common objections during the meeting. Understanding the most frequent concerns and having well-thought-out responses can help you navigate the conversation more effectively.

5. Increase Deal Size

- **Upsell and Cross-Sell**: Identify opportunities to upsell or cross-sell additional products or services. If a prospect is interested in one solution, explain how complementary products can enhance the value or solve additional problems.

- **Tiered Pricing**: Offer tiered pricing packages that provide higher value at different levels. This allows prospects to choose a package that fits their budget while still increasing the overall deal size.

- **Highlight Long-Term Benefits**: Emphasize the long-term benefits and ROI of your solution. Help prospects see the bigger picture and how a larger investment now can lead to greater savings or revenue in the future.

By focusing on these five areas—doubling the number of emails sent, improving open and response rates, converting more appointments to sales, and increasing deal size—you can strategically double your income through cold emailing. Each step involves a combination of personalization, automation, data-driven decision-making, and a clear value proposition to maximize your effectiveness and results.

PRE-WORK

N ot everyone is prepared to send cold emails right away. So, let's make sure you're prepared. One of the most serious difficulties I've seen with cold email is that businesses would attempt it without the fundamentals in place. Cold email will not work properly until you have everything in order. And then, you won't receive the desired results, and you could decide to stop using cold email altogether. Or determining that cold email is either spam or useless. That would be a terrible waste.

Businesses fail to include three critical components of a successful cold email offer. The three components are case studies, the offer, and the target market.

Case Studies

First, get your case studies perfectly aligned. You want to provide an offer that potential clients will find irresistible. Most importantly, you want the target market to be able to afford your offer. This is because cold email is not the same as inbound email; you are effectively driving the process. So you'll need to do 90% of the effort and pitch a proposition rather than a service.

I will give you an example.

An agency will compose a cold email which will say something like this:

Subject: *Quick Questions*

Hi, Mark.

Are you interested in doing any web development projects?

We specialize in many languages and can create websites and apps as well.

Let me know your thoughts.

Regards,

John Doe

This email is junk. Why? That is pitching a service, not an offer. Pitching an offer entails creating something that a buyer can buy. For example:

Subject: *Quick Questions*

Hey Karen, I'm a major fan of your work with Acme Tours – especially the last video!

I specialize in composing emails for tour businesses. Recently, one client improved their revenue by 71% with just one newsletter. I would want to do the same for you. Is that anything you're interested in?

Thanks,

John Doe

That is how any company sending cold emails should pitch. Instead of simply informing the customer that they do copywriting, tell them who you deal with as a copywriting agency and how you have produced excellent outcomes, and then offer to do the same for them.

Here is an example from the realm of app development.

Subject: *Quick Questions*

Hello Brian, John Doe again in Boca Raton – a major fan of the city!

We just completed a new project with the City of San Diego Treasury Department, where we developed a bespoke application that calculates how much tax is owed to the city and a back-office system that allows Treasury offices to collect taxes more effectively.

I would love to discuss rewriting your tax collection software to help you optimize your procedures and add new features.

Would you be interested? Drop me a line, and we'll set up a call for you.

Regards,

John Doe

Again, this promotes a specific service to provide specialized tax collection software for city Treasury departments. This is only one example; the corporation can pitch *specific* app development or technology products, but not *any*.

Another example might be a company that sells pay-per-click ads, which is a massive market. Their email might read like this:

Subject: *Quick Questions*

Hello, Samia.

Congratulations on your six-year tenure with Acme Residential!

We've been running Google advertising for 12 years and have filled over 11,000 beds in rehab facilities nationwide. I would want to do the same for you. Let's chat.

Thanks,

John Doe

Another specialized pitch involves providing a clearly defined service. Finally, here's an example of social media marketing:

Subject: *Quick Questions*

Hey Roger, congratulations on getting the Best of Las Vegas award! I figured you'd enjoy this:

Over the previous few years, I've grown dozens of Instagram profiles for realtors, and my focus is on discovering new customers rather than building followers.

I would want to do the same for you. Let's chat.

Thanks,

John Doe

Note how precise these deals are. We don't sell "social media" but rather "Instagram growth for lawyers." Other than "web & mobile design," rather "tax collection software for City Treasury Departments." The objective is to condense your case studies into one-sentence proposals before sending cold emails. Make them hyper-specific. It is not enough to simply target a specific industry; they must also address a specific problem.

Ideally, your pitch is something that has previously improved income for organizations, which you can mention in your email. Remember: sugar, salt, and fat. We are like McDonald's. Deliver that value by promising to make them money, just like McDonald's claims to make you feel good by serving you sugar, salt, and fat!

One crucial element to remember is that your case study should appeal to companies comparable to the ones you previously sold to. So, the earlier sale mentioned in your case study cannot be too explicit. I know I just said it had to be specialized, but it also needed to be generalizable to the rest of the market. You must be precise enough that someone in that market would quickly recognize the benefits yet general enough that it can be applied to many organizations.

Review the scripts mentioned in the email again; they strike the ideal balance between being industry-specific and buyable by multiple companies.

And I'd like to underline the importance of finding an acceptable niche. Any company earns between $5 million and $150 million in revenue. Companies in this category have the money to pay for and are not burdened by the layers of administration and decision-making common in large corporations.

Companies at this level are willing to spend $50,000 on a project and have it approved within a few days. A mom-and-pop store may approve a proposal in a few days but only pay $200. And while an enterprise may be eager to pay you $50,000 or more, the project may take six months to get approved.

So, you want to make sure that your target market meets the requirements of severely needing your services and being able to purchase them.

You can determine your target market based on current case studies. If you have previously performed admirably for a major hospital, you can now market to other significant hospitals. If a nonprofit buys a logo you created, you may now target other nonprofits. And so on.

Finally, if you don't have any case studies, you may not be ready for cold email just yet. That is the cold, brutal reality. However, you can borrow case studies from other agencies if you are beginning from scratch. This requires contacting a current agency and requesting to become a partner.

That is a good offer.

An excellent offer is specific and related to a financial aim. This means that when someone hears your offer for the first time, they will immediately realize that it will increase their income or make them appear good at work. Ideally, money is preferable because when you consider what McDonald's does — it is by no means the best fast food in the world, but it has sugar, salt, and fat. Making more money is the business world's sweet, salty, and fatty. If you can offer that to someone, it's extremely simple to sell.

With this in mind, I try to reframe everything we offer in terms of how much money it will generate for our potential clients. If you design logos, you may help build brand credibility, leading to greater sales. If you construct a website, you will either boost overall consumer satisfaction or conversion rate, resulting in more sales. Instead of simply writing words, copywriters create mailing blasts or blogs that lead directly to increased sales.

This allows you to construct a no-brainer offer. Something so beneficial to the organization that it would be foolish to refuse. And they believe in you because you can illustrate your previous successes. A good example of a no-brainer offer is:

I will create three newsletters for you, and if you do not make more money than you paid for my services, I will refund your money.

<u>Another good no-brainer offer:</u>

I will analyze all of your Facebook ad campaigns, and if we do not uncover at least two optimizations that increase your revenue, you will no longer be required to work with us. But if we locate them, let's scale your ads.

<u>More examples of no-brainer offers</u>

Facebook advertisements: Manage ads for 30 days; if there is no return on investment, we will refund your fee.

Newsletter copywriting: Write three newsletters for a 50% commission; no sales, no cash.

Lead generation (Outbound): Schedule 10 meetings in 4 weeks or get your money back.

Website design: just wireframes; we'll refund your money if you don't like where this is going.

Mobile app development: wireframes just; you can get your money back if you don't like where this is going.

Backend development: A two-hour tech review; we can terminate the contract after that if you do not see the benefit.

Branding: Let's just create a mood board; if you don't like where this is going, we can refund.

Search Engine Optimization: In-depth review (not the kind that other people give for free). If you are dissatisfied, we will refund your purchase.

Domain Name

Okay, we have the case study and offer drilled down. We now need to choose a domain name. Now, you are thinking. "We already have a domain name, and it's ideal for our business! We do not need a new domain name! "Why on earth would we need to consider this?"

That's an entirely true observation, but there's a reason! You already use your current domain name to communicate with the rest of the world. The most obvious example of this would be Google.com, which is well-known to almost everyone worldwide. Google values its brand and does not want to jeopardize it in any way.

On a smaller scale, you may eventually attain Google's income, but anything is possible. You must secure your domain name and online identity as if your life depended on them. In some circumstances, your life depends on it!

One potential difficulty with cold email is that it may be classed as spam, causing complications for your existing domain.

You're probably thinking right now. I thought we weren't spamming?! Sure, but like with any new talent, you will undoubtedly make blunders when starting out with a cold email. If you expect to come into a cold email and have everything 100% correct immediately, it is not impossible, but it is unlikely.

However, there is a simple solution to this difficulty. You simply buy domain names that are comparable to your current domain. Because if you send out 3,000 cold emails on a whim and they are tagged as spam, it is the end of your domain. This might be a complete disaster for your company, especially if it is relatively well-established. Consider internal corporate communications that end up in the spam folder, customer bills that fail to arrive, and so on. Protect your main domain name like it's a golden banner.

COLD EMAIL SUCCESS IN 24 HOURS

The simplest method to avoid this potential problem is to use similar domains. So, purchase numerous domain names similar to your current domain name and redirect them to your existing websites.

Redirecting is not difficult to perform; just look for it on Google. It's worth noting that many large corporations have done this, including changing their primary domain in some situations. Everyone does this! It's common for businesses to sell from non-standard domain names, so make sure you follow this procedure.

Target Audience

Email Signature

You must adequately calibrate your inbox to write the perfect cold email. This includes setting up the signature. This is very crucial. In case you didn't know, the signature is at the bottom of your cold email. It appears to be benign, but most people get it incorrect.

Email signatures with large photos, a variety of text, or 20 separate links to different elements of your firm are more detrimental than beneficial. These are all approaches you should avoid. A smart email signature includes only your Name, contact information, and one compelling link. Clean, uncomplicated, and effective.

Here's a template:

[Your Name] | [Your Job Title]

[Your Phone Number]

[Your Email Address]

Learn more about our new offerings: [Link to a Relevant Landing Page]

Another key point is that photographs result in more manual spam complaints. Therefore, the fewer graphics you have in your email, the better. In many circumstances, including an avatar or image of oneself can detract from your cold email.

"Why?" I hear you asking! Perhaps you appear too much like a model. Perhaps you don't appear like a model enough (this is a common problem). Perhaps the individual to whom you're writing the email has certain predetermined notions that they are unaware of. The point is that including your photo can only make matters worse. You are getting nothing while perhaps losing a lot. Similarly, by giving images and links, we encourage visitors to browse our website before booking a meeting and purchasing our product or service. As a result, they bring little value and may even detract from the purpose of the activity.

There is a standard template you can use for your signature.

- First line: First Name, last Name, and title.
- Second line: Company name.
- On the third line, provide your office address.
- Fourth line: The best phone number.
- Fifth line: Email and website.

Setting Up The Inbox And Authentication

But you aren't ready to send cold emails just yet! You must set up your inbox correctly. This is more significant than you might think. Spam filters are becoming increasingly intelligent, so failing to calibrate your inbox appropriately is the simplest way to get flagged as spam. As a result, the entire operation will be rendered useless, if not harmful. So, make sure you set up your email inbox correctly.

To begin, enter all of the information requested on the account setup form. This includes uploading a profile photo and providing your first, surname, and address information. Also, make sure you have everything set up in your G Suite. Because Google automatically verifies all of this. If it is not correctly completed, it will be counted against you.

The next step in the process is to authenticate your email. Before I continue, I'd want to issue a little warning. This could potentially change in the future. I tried to make sure that everything in this book was totally future-proof, but there is one example of helpful something now that could evolve in the coming years.

DMARC allows you to send emails at scale without being flagged as spam. It's a verification system that Google and several other large providers employ. It is not a license to spam everyone and everyone, but it has been created to help receivers make better decisions about domain reputations. DMARC provides a platform for senders to publish policies that guard against spam and phishing, hence improving domain reputations.

This is a little complex, but DMARC is essentially a website's SSL. It's an identity that lends credibility to a specific email platform. SSL is related to the HTTPS predecessor, which I'm sure everyone listening to this book has come across on the Internet. This mechanism ensures that malicious individuals cannot just set up phony domains online and have them considered authentic. Https generates a verification symbol in the top left corner of your browser, indicating that pages are safe. DMARC essentially serves the same purpose as email.

However, the best approach moving forward is to Google "how to add DMARC." That way, whatever information you find will always be up to date.

Warming Up the Email

If you've followed everything so far, you'll have set up your email account, calibrated your signature, and configured DMARC so that you're not flagged as spam. Finally, to avoid the spam box, Google must trust that you are legitimate. You know you're real, but Google can still say you're not!

New customers should not sign up for a service and send thousands of emails without a response. This is a certain method to get designated as spam right away. Spam filters will immediately identify you as a spammer; no one will ever read your emails, and you will have to go through the entire process of creating a new email mailbox. Which I'm sure you'd want to avoid!

Fortunately, automatic tools can warm up your inbox for you. There are a number of these available at coldemailmanifesto.com/tools. These connect your email to a network of other email inboxes, which continuously transfer messages back and forth. It will also generate content, demonstrating to Google that your inbox is not spammy. It warms up your domain, ensuring that cold emails are delivered to the Primary mailbox rather than Spam or Promotions folders. This can be done manually, but I would definitely advocate using tools to make the process more simple and faster.

LEAD GENERATION

You've already done a lot of preparation. You've done the groundwork, have your case studies, know where you want to position yourself in the market and know who you want to target. And your thinking should be in the right place to begin taking advantage of cold emails.

But before we go any further, let's talk about lead generation. This may not be particularly fascinating to you, but it is critical to establish a network of qualified contacts. These people are most likely to respond and buy from your company.

To whom you send an email campaign is more crucial than the email's content.

Let me repeat that.

To whom you send an email campaign is more crucial than the email's content.

You will likely receive a response even if you submit a badly thought-out proposal to a clean contact list of Fortune 500 CEOs. However, sending the same second-quality pitch to an unclean list with a high bounce rate will result in spam. And it is never where we want to be!

Avoiding Irrelevant Emails

But before we go any further, let me address an obvious question. Why is this important? Why can't you simply send emails to anybody and everyone? You can do this if you want, but if you send emails to people who aren't interested, you'll get considerably lower response rates and risk landing in spam. This is something you should avoid at all costs. And if you send people irrelevant emails, even if you've properly warmed up your inbox and have the best cold email in the world, you may still be called spam. The more improper contacts you bombard with irrelevant emails, the more likely you will destroy your email account.

A cold email is not spam; don't turn it into one. So, you must have stringent lead generation requirements. This will ensure that your entire operation is above board and that you are useful rather than a nuisance. Lead generation is not about sending out as many emails as possible; rather, it is about discovering people who require your services and, more importantly, can afford to pay your desired price.

To achieve this, we must establish lead generation criteria. The first step in this process is to go over some of the requirements for sending effective cold emails. These include the first and last Name, email address, website, company name, and a personalized first line. You only need five data points for each lead.

All of this information is available online, except for the personalized first line, which you must obviously write yourself! However, we must first define our target market to identify this information. And there are three requirements: a certain industry, job title, and company size.

Targeting the Industry

Starting with the industry, you should tackle it based on your case study and become quite detailed. We discussed pre-work and narrowing down your case studies in the previous chapter. So, you can now utilize the case study to determine who will buy from you. And it's critical to get down to the specifics of what you're attempting to do. As already stated, eCommerce is not adequate. Instead, it should be specific – subscription boxes, clothes, tool manufacturers, or whatever meets your specific requirements. You don't only look for startups but also B2B, SaaS, consumer apps, machine learning, and anything else that fits your business model.

Many people make a rookie mistake early on by thinking they're marketing to all businesses, while B2B and B2C startups are fundamentally different.

Even within particular niches, a pre-traction B2C firm with $500 million in cash is not comparable to a bootstrapped B2C with thousands of established clients. Although they are fundamentally distinct enterprises, both are sometimes referred to as startups. As a result, you must distinguish between the organizations you are targeting and choose which ones will be most suitable for your specific business.

This strategy allows you to make even the most esoteric pitches to the most niche sectors. For example, we generated leads for an event management startup at one point. The entire industry is dependent on people who organize major events. However, identifying these individuals is difficult because no database of event organizers existed at the time.

Case Study

So, our initial step was to create a lead pool. To accomplish this, compiled a list of the top events and then narrowed it down to simply New York City (where this agency was situated). We then worked our way backward through the list to uncover the organizers' names and contact information. Only at this point were we allowed to email these individuals and begin scheduling meetings.

The best part about contacting folks in niche businesses is that no one else can identify them! So they aren't disturbed too much! In many ways, targeting niche and very particular sectors is preferable because they receive significantly less contact. You can even think outside the box by attending conferences and events that allow you to interact with the people you want to reach.

The main thing to understand is that you cannot limit what you can do using cold email. There are no limitations or goals that you cannot pursue. You may have to be imaginative, but this entire method can connect you with anyone or anything.

Job Titles

Once you've decided on an industry, the second thing you need to consider is the job title. I'm sure you'll agree that setting high goals in this department is logical. I nearly always start with the CEO since it is ideal to go directly to the top right away. You probably want to stop me right there. You might say, "You're intending to sell to a major enterprise, and it's obviously pointless to email the CEO of Morgan Stanley, as he's never going to respond." Nothing is impossible. Yes, there will be occasions when you do not receive the desired response, but you may adjust your expectations accordingly. If you don't set ambitious goals from the start, you'll never know if you'll succeed.

If the CEO does not respond, work your way down the corporate command structure, one title at a time, every two weeks. Target the Chief Marketing Officer, followed by the Director of Marketing, the Senior Brand Manager, and finally, the Associate Brand Manager. Emailing two people from the same company simultaneously is also not a good idea. Only deal with one contact at a time; otherwise, you risk spamming them. Or two people could see your email, show it to each other, and then realize it's a mass email, lowering your response rate and increasing your chance of spam!

I discovered that, particularly in offices, it is preferable to have the Director of Marketing introduce you to the Director of Technology and then engage in an organic conversation. The alternative is for the Director of Marketing and the Director of Technology to discuss your communication and conclude that you've been spamming them both. It is preferable to email only one person and have them be the only one in the firm who discovers your services and value.

Company Size

The third crucial factor is the size of the company. As previously indicated, you can target Golden Geese enterprises with yearly revenues ranging from $5 million to $150 million. However, I want to highlight once more that smaller enterprises and local commerce can be addressed, although they are more difficult to close large deals with. You can also sell to large organizations. However, the process is lengthier and more difficult. That is why Golden Geese firms are the ideal to collaborate with. They have more money than a small business but lack the complexity of a large management and organizational structure.

Lead Scraping

Lead scraping is the earliest approach for generating leads and is laborious. This essentially means that you conduct web research to compile a list of organizations from which to construct your email list. For example, you might look for top airlines or use LinkedIn to find people who meet a given requirement.

Then, you run a lead scraping tool that extracts and generates data from the website in a document. These tools allow you to verify emails, which minimizes your bounce rate. All of this is necessary to make the process as efficient as possible while maintaining your email inbox's credibility.

Then, you would send emails depending on the manual leads that were harvested during this procedure. This is not necessarily the best technique to create leads, but it is certainly the most cost-effective. Lead scraping appeals to many beginners, and I wouldn't necessarily discourage it if you're on a small budget. However, I do not normally endorse this strategy because hiring people who are intimately familiar with lead creation yields far superior outcomes.

Web Scraping Tools

Web scraping tools are software applications designed to extract large amounts of data from websites. They can access web pages, identify the relevant information, and store this data in a structured format like a spreadsheet or database. This allows businesses to gather contact information, such as email addresses, phone numbers, and other relevant details from multiple sources quickly and efficiently.

Benefits of Using Web Scraping Tools

1. Efficiency and Speed: Web scraping tools can process large volumes of data much faster than manual methods. This efficiency allows you to build comprehensive email lists in a fraction of the time it would take to do manually. If you need to collect email addresses from hundreds of company websites, a web scraping tool can automate this task and complete it within hours, whereas manual data collection might take days or even weeks.

2. Accuracy and Consistency: These tools are designed to extract data accurately and consistently. Automating the process reduces the risk of human error, such as typos or missing information, ensuring that the data you collect is reliable and uniform. Using a tool like Octoparse, you can set specific criteria for the data you want to extract, ensuring that only relevant and accurate information is collected from each website.

3. Scalability: Web scraping tools can handle large-scale data extraction tasks, making it easy to scale your email list as your business grows. Whether you need to scrape data from a few websites or thousands, these tools can manage the workload efficiently. A growing business can use web scraping tools to continually expand its email list by regularly extracting data from new websites and updating its database with fresh leads.

4. Customization: Many web scraping tools offer customization options, allowing you to tailor the data extraction process to your specific needs. You can set parameters for what data to collect, from which sections of the website, and how to structure the output. With a tool like Scrapy, you can write custom scripts to extract data from specific fields on a webpage, such as names, job titles, and email addresses, and format this data into a structured CSV file for easy import into your CRM.

5. Cost-Effective: While some web scraping tools require a subscription fee, the cost is often offset by the time and labor savings they provide. Automated data collection is more cost-effective than hiring additional staff to gather information manually. A subscription to a web scraping service like Import.io may cost a few hundred dollars annually, but this expense is justified by the large volume of high-quality data it can collect, leading to increased sales and business growth.

Popular Web Scraping Tools

1. Scrapy is an open-source web crawling framework for Python that allows you to build and run web spiders to extract data from websites. It is highly customizable and suitable for complex scraping tasks.

Key Features:

- High-level data extraction with minimal code
- Built-in support for handling different data formats
- Robust and scalable, capable of scraping large volumes of data
- Extensive documentation and active community support

Use Case: Ideal for businesses with technical expertise looking to build custom web scraping solutions for specific data extraction needs.

2. Octoparse is a user-friendly web scraping tool that requires no coding skills. It provides a visual interface for setting up data extraction tasks and supports both simple and complex scraping scenarios.

Key Features:

- Drag-and-drop interface for easy setup
- Pre-built templates for common scraping tasks
- Cloud-based scraping for large-scale data extraction
- Data export in various formats, including CSV, Excel, and databases

Use Case: Suitable for businesses of all sizes that need a straightforward and efficient solution for web scraping without the need for programming knowledge.

3. Import.io is a web data integration tool that converts web pages into structured data. It offers desktop and cloud-based web scraping solutions, making it accessible for different business needs.

Key Features:

- Point-and-click interface for easy data extraction
- API integration for automated data retrieval
- Real-time data extraction and updates
- Support for a wide range of data formats and export options

Use Case: Best for businesses looking for a reliable and versatile web scraping tool that can handle various data extraction requirements and integrate seamlessly with other systems.

Lead Databases

One of the most effective tactics for any organization, regardless of budget, is to use the numerous lead-generation databases accessible today. These databases can greatly improve your cold emailing efforts by supplying you with high-quality leads that are personalized to your unique requirements.

Lead-generating databases provide various information that can help you locate and contact new clients. These tools enable you to search for leads based on various factors, including industry, firm size, revenue, location, and more. This customized method ensures that your cold emails are delivered to the intended recipients, improving the likelihood of a positive response.

Benefits of Using Lead Generation Databases

Lead generation databases offer numerous advantages that can significantly enhance your cold emailing efforts. Below, we delve deeper into the key benefits of using these powerful tools.

Targeted Outreach: Lead generation databases allow you to filter and segment your potential contacts based on a wide range of criteria, such as industry, company size, revenue, location, and job title. This targeted approach ensures that your emails are sent to the most relevant recipients, who are more likely to be interested in your products or services.

Example: If you are selling software solutions for small businesses in the healthcare industry, you can use a lead generation database to find healthcare companies with fewer than 50 employees. This targeted list helps you avoid wasting time and resources on contacts that are unlikely to convert.

Time Efficiency: Manually searching for leads can be an incredibly time-consuming process. Lead generation databases streamline this task by providing a centralized platform where you can quickly compile a list of potential contacts. This efficiency allows you to focus more on crafting personalized emails and other core business activities.

Example: Instead of spending hours researching and collecting contact information from various sources, you can use a tool like ZoomInfo to generate a list of hundreds of qualified leads within minutes.

Data Accuracy: Reputable lead generation databases regularly update their information to ensure accuracy. This means that the contact details you obtain are up-to-date, reducing the chances of your emails bouncing or reaching the wrong person. Accurate data is crucial for maintaining a good sender reputation and ensuring high deliverability rates.

Example: Using an outdated contact list can result in a high bounce rate, negatively impacting your email deliverability and sender reputation. A database like LinkedIn Sales Navigator provides current data, helping you avoid these issues.

Enhanced Personalization: Detailed information about your leads allows you to tailor your emails to each recipient's specific needs and interests.

Personalization is key to making your emails stand out and resonate with your audience, leading to higher engagement and conversion rates.

Example: If you know the recipient's job title and recent company achievements, you can craft a personalized email that addresses their specific challenges and how your product or service can help them achieve their goals.

Scalability: Lead generation databases enable you to scale your outreach efforts efficiently. Whether you need to contact hundreds or thousands of potential leads, these tools can handle large volumes of data and provide the necessary resources to support your campaigns.

Example: A small business looking to expand its market reach can quickly scale its lead generation efforts using a database like Hunter.io, which allows for bulk email searches and exports.

Competitive Advantage: Access to high-quality lead generation databases gives you a competitive edge by enabling you to reach potential customers faster and more effectively than your competitors. You can stay ahead in your industry by leveraging the latest tools and technologies.

Example: By using advanced filtering options and real-time data updates, you can identify and reach out to high-potential leads before your competitors do, increasing your chances of winning new business.

Cost-Effective: While some lead generation databases require a subscription fee, their high-quality leads and time savings often justify the cost. Investing in a reliable database can yield a significant return on investment by improving your campaign results and reducing manual effort.

Example: A monthly subscription to a service like ZoomInfo may cost a few hundred dollars, but its high-quality leads can lead to new sales and long-term customer relationships that far outweigh the initial investment.

Key Features to Look For

When choosing a lead-generating database, consider the following qualities to enhance your cold emailing success:

- **Industry and Revenue Search:** Ensure the tool lets you filter leads by industry and revenue. This assists in identifying firms that are most likely to profit from your products or services.

- **Advanced Filtering Options:** Look for databases that include a variety of filtering choices, including company size, geography, job title, and more. The more specific the filters, the more targeted your outreach will be.

- **Bespoke First Line Writing:** Some top solutions allow you to personalize and engage your emails with bespoke first lines. This function is especially handy if you're new to cold emailing and want to make an excellent first impression.

- **Integrated Email Sending:** Some programs let you send emails directly from the platform. This can improve your productivity and allow you to manage your campaigns more effectively.

Test a few options to see which suits your needs and preferences best. Once you've chosen a tool, use its features to create a targeted list of leads and begin crafting your cold emails.

Lead generation databases ensure your outreach is focused, personalized, and effective. Remember that the key to effective cold emailing is your emails' content and your leads' quality and relevance. To get the best results from your cold emailing campaigns, use these databases, stay current on the latest tools, and constantly fine-tune your approach.

Popular Lead Generation Databases

1. LinkedIn Sales Navigator is a premium tool that provides advanced search and filtering options to help you find leads based on specific criteria.

Key Features:

- Advanced lead and company search filters
- Real-time insights and updates about leads
- Integration with CRM systems
- InMail messaging for direct communication with leads

Use Case: Ideal for B2B businesses looking to target professionals based on job title, industry, and company size.

2. ZoomInfo is a comprehensive lead generation platform that offers detailed information about businesses and professionals, including contact details, company data, and industry insights.

Key Features:

- Extensive database of business contacts
- Advanced search filters and segmentation options
- Integration with popular CRM and marketing automation tools
- Real-time data updates and enrichment

Use Case: Suitable for businesses of all sizes that need accurate and detailed information to build targeted email lists.

3. Hunter.io is an email finder tool that helps you locate email addresses associated with specific domains and verify their validity.

Key Features:

- Domain search to find email addresses from a specific company
- Email verification to ensure deliverability
- Bulk email search and export options
- Integration with CRM and outreach tools

Use Case: Useful for businesses looking to find and verify email addresses quickly and efficiently.

Lead generation databases are invaluable tools for businesses looking to streamline their cold emailing campaigns and reach the right audience. By providing access to detailed and accurate information about potential leads, these databases enable targeted outreach, save time, and enhance the personalization of your emails. Incorporate lead generation databases into your cold emailing strategy to maximize your chances of success and achieve better results.

Online Freelancers

The third most valuable source of leads is online freelancers. Numerous job boards are available online, and Upwork is currently the most well-known. These platforms can be used to hire a freelancer to help you generate leads. Job boards are fantastic because they are used by people all over the globe.

They are becoming more credible, so you can hire lead generators trained by the world's top companies, including Salesforce, Cisco Systems, Oracle, and others that excel at outreach.

This allows you to obtain a low-cost, verified list of emails that are ready to use out of the box. I typically hire 3-4 freelancers and test their emails with an email verification tool. This helps me determine which ones are legitimate, and if we discover that one or two of the people we've hired have done an excellent job, we'll hire them permanently.

In some cases, the lead quality may be extremely low, but if the hire fails to deliver, you may be eligible for a refund. It's difficult to recommend pricing for this particular task, as it can vary greatly depending on the market and the people that you hire. I can say that there is a huge number of people available who can offer value in lead generation, and you can negotiate and bring them on board at a price point that makes sense for your company and the person you're hiring.

Lead generation is an important part of the cold email process. Ensuring your operation is efficient is critical and helps prevent your email inbox from becoming spammy. It can be done relatively inexpensively, and investing that money to get the desired results is worthwhile.

Generally speaking, cutting corners in life doesn't work, and it definitely doesn't work with cold email. You do need to invest some due diligence into the process if you want great results. As with so many things in life, you will only get out of cold email what you put into it in the first place, so get to work!

Email Finder Tools

Email finder tools are specialized software applications designed to help businesses locate and verify email addresses. These tools are particularly useful in cold emailing campaigns, where having accurate contact information is crucial for reaching potential leads effectively.

Email finder tools are online services or software that allow you to find email addresses associated with specific domains, companies, or individuals. These tools use various algorithms and databases to locate email addresses and often include verification features to ensure the validity of the email addresses they find.

Benefits of Using Email Finder Tools

1. Accuracy: Email finder tools provide accurate and verified email addresses, reducing the risk of sending emails to invalid or non-existent addresses. This ensures that your emails reach the intended recipients, improving your email deliverability and response rates.

A tool like Hunter.io cross-references multiple sources to verify email addresses, providing high accuracy and reducing the chances of bounce rates.

2. Efficiency: These tools can quickly find email addresses from large databases or websites, saving you the time and effort required to search for contact information manually. This efficiency allows you to compile large lists of email addresses in a short amount of time.

Using Voila Norbert, you can input a company domain and receive a list of associated email addresses within minutes, streamlining the process of building your email list.

3. Integration: Many email finder tools integrate seamlessly with other tools and platforms, such as CRM systems, email marketing software, and productivity applications. This integration allows for smooth data transfer and streamlined workflows.

Clearbit Connect integrates with Gmail, allowing you to find and verify email addresses directly from your email client and making adding contacts to your email campaigns easy.

4. Customization: Email finder tools often provide various search and filtering options, allowing you to customize your searches based on specific criteria. This customization helps you find the most relevant contacts for your cold emailing campaigns.

FindThatLead allows you to filter searches by industry, job title, location, and more, ensuring that you find email addresses that match your target audience.

5. Cost-Effective: Investing in an email finder tool can be cost-effective, especially when compared to the cost of manually searching for email addresses or dealing with high bounce rates due to inaccurate contact information.

The subscription cost for an email finder tool like Hunter.io can be justified by the increase in successful email deliveries and conversions resulting from accurate contact information.

Popular Email Finder Tools

1. Voila Norbert is an email finder and verification tool that helps you locate email addresses and validate their accuracy. It is known for its simplicity and effectiveness.

Key Features:

- Find and verify email addresses with high accuracy
- Bulk email search capabilities
- Integration with CRM and email marketing platforms
- User-friendly interface

Use Case: Suitable for businesses of all sizes that need a reliable tool for finding and verifying email addresses for their outreach efforts.

2. FindThatLead is an email finder tool that helps you locate email addresses based on various criteria, such as domain, social profiles, or other specific filters. It also offers email verification services.

Key Features:

- Advanced search filters by industry, job title, location, and more
- Email verification to ensure accuracy
- Integration with popular CRM and marketing tools
- Bulk email search and export options

Use Case: Best for businesses looking for a comprehensive solution to find and verify email addresses based on specific criteria.

4. Clearbit Connect is a Gmail extension that helps you find email addresses and provides contextual information about contacts. It is designed to work directly within your email client for seamless integration.

Key Features:

- Find email addresses from within Gmail
- View detailed contact information and company data
- Integration with CRM and productivity tools
- Real-time data updates

Use Case: Ideal for businesses and individuals wanting to find and verify email addresses without leaving their clients.

How to Use Email Finder Tools

- Identify Target Domains or Individuals: Determine the companies or individuals you want to contact. This can be based on your target market, industry, or specific criteria relevant to your campaign.
- Input Information into the Tool: Use the email finder tool to search for email addresses by entering domain names, company names, or individual names. Customize your search using available filters to narrow down the results.

- Verify Email Addresses: Once you have a list of potential email addresses, use the tool's verification feature to check the validity of each address. This step is crucial to ensure that your emails reach the intended recipients and reduce bounce rates.
- Export and Organize Data: Export and organize the verified email addresses in your CRM system or email marketing platform. This will help you manage your contacts and streamline your outreach efforts.
- Personalize Your Emails: Use the detailed information the email finder tool provides to personalize your cold emails. Tailor your messages to the specific needs and interests of each recipient to increase engagement and response rates.
- Monitor and Adjust: Track the performance of your email campaigns and make necessary adjustments based on the feedback and data you receive. Use the insights gained to refine your approach and improve future campaigns.

Email finder tools are essential for businesses compiling accurate and comprehensive email lists for their cold emailing campaigns. Incorporate email finder tools into your strategy to ensure that your emails reach the right people, improve your deliverability rates, and achieve better results in your marketing campaigns.

THE PERFECT COLD EMAIL

T his chapter is the most essential in the book. This is where I'll explain the structure of a perfect cold email. The five components work together to form a structure that will earn you serious money.

I'll also show you some email examples that have worked for me and our clients. By the end of this chapter, you'll be able to draft your own excellent cold email, which you can test immediately. This will be an action-packed chapter, so I hope you are prepared to work!

Buying from Strangers

But first, I want you to ask yourself an essential question. What would it take for you to buy from a stranger? That is an extremely crucial question because that is essentially what you are doing here. Contacting someone out of the blue with a proposition when they know virtually nothing about you. So you have to be convincing. You have to get their attention quickly.

Remember this principle when composing a cold email because it will ultimately determine your success. After you've captured your potential client's attention, the following step is to portray authority. This can be accomplished by providing excellent value early, breaking through all of the noise and worries that will undoubtedly be swirling around this customer's mind. Your aim with cold email is to remove these doubts.

Make the consumer believe that they merely need to contact you. Not all of these first interactions will lead to sales, but achieving the percentages outlined in the book will undoubtedly create more business.

This process stage is addressed by the three components of the cold email that I outlined earlier: praise, a case study, and a call to action. The compliment captures their attention, the case study establishes authority, and the call to action encourages them to schedule a meeting. And it's all done in three sentences. That doesn't seem very labor-intensive, does it?

Okay, let us go through some examples. This is a script for mobile development.

Subject: *Quick question. Jack*

Hello, Jack.

I am a huge fan of Acme Inc. and your innovative marketing technique!

Recently, I assisted several companies in developing VR applications to increase brand awareness, and I would be delighted to do the same for you.

Do you mind if I send it over several times for a short call?

Thanks,

John Doe

It's vital to note that this company is incredibly particular. Drill down into something you know is important to the client. Don't just tell them you do app development; everyone does it, so what?

Here's another example of a pay-per-click marketing campaign:

Subject: *Quick question*

Hello, Greg.

I hope your day is going well so far - I just discovered Acme and thought I'd contact you.

Globonet, a technology business, recently used email, LinkedIn advertising, and content marketing to promote their product, resulting in 500+ leads and $2M in sales in a year.

I'd love to help you do something similar for Acme; okay if I send you a couple of messages to chat?

Thanks,
John Doe

Another Example of Brand Strategy

Subject: *Call next week?*

Hello, Jackson.

I discovered Acme recently and fell in love with it!

Globonet's website and marketing materials were recently completed, and the company saw a 97% rise in mobile visits per year. I'd love to do the same and help elevate the Acme brand to the next level.

Do you mind if I email along some available times for a call next week?

Best regards,
John Doe

It's a really basic process, but completing all the steps is critical. So, let's get started on creating the ultimate cold email.

Subject Line

The logical place to begin is with the topic line. But why is this so important? Simply said, your subject line is the initial point of contact with a potential prospect. It's the first thing they see in their email, and they'll judge you based on that. They will only see this and your Name, so make it excellent. This is the factor that determines whether your email is opened or deleted.

In a moment, we'll provide you with some excellent instances. But first, remember that an excellent subject line is direct. It is short and to the point. You frequently interact with incredibly busy people, and you must create an immediate impression on them. Furthermore, the entire message will not be shown in the email inbox if your subject line is too long.

Your subject line should be no more than five words, preferably two. It must pique the recipient's interest to the point that they are forced to click it.

It is acceptable to use clickbait in this context! You want them to consider what it could be but cannot determine without opening the email.

Finally, many effective topic lines will be individualized. This isn't always the case, and our most popular subject line immediately breaches this rule! Other personalized options include the recipient's Name, company name, or other unique identifiers. Again, this distinguishes your email from those that will be considered spam and shows that it is truly addressed to the recipient.

But, to make things easier for you, I'm going to give you our top ten most successful subject lines right now:

- Quick Question

- [Name], Quick Question
- Quick Question, [Company Name]
- <Relevant emoji>
- Question?
- Something for you, [Name]
- Interview Invite
- I've got a Story for You
- [Name] Recommended I Get in Touch
- Intro

"Quick Question" is unquestionably the most effective subject line. However, testing some other examples is important since you may get different results in your field. I should clarify that the emoji-based example was chosen since we were pitching to game developers; you should use something relevant to another industry. The emoji vary according to the offer and recipient, so experiment and find what works best for you. For example, a beer emoji was effective when we sold to breweries.

Personalized First Line

The second step in the procedure is to generate a great tailored first line. Again, the goal is to get the receiver to respond. As previously said, this is based on a personalized compliment. This isn't always the easiest thing to write and can be uncomfortable. However, it is just the most effective method of communicating with clients.

I am sure the notion of drafting individualized cold emails is not appealing. You might wish to skip this section. We all do. Nobody wants to put in the effort of creating individualized cold emails; I barely want to do it!

We only employ this method because it is ten times more effective than not personalizing. If we could avoid personalizing, we would surely skip the entire procedure. There are occasions when you narrow down sufficiently; you can write a first line that appeals to everyone in your niche or develop a first line with one personalized data piece that you can outsource. For example, for cosmetics, you might write:

Hello, Jack. My partner expressed her enthusiasm for {!Company name}, particularly the {!Product Name}, so I decided to contact them directly.

If you can't find a system like that, a custom complement can help you stand out among the potentially thousands of other communications important people receive. It will identify you as the wheat to be separated from the chaff. So it's definitely worth taking a few minutes to get the wheels in motion for agreements worth tens of thousands, if not hundreds of thousands of dollars. It just makes sense.

A unique complement may be comparable to the million-dollar email script that we previously discussed:

"I've been following Fuzz for a long time, and I enjoy your work. Great job at the Rockefeller Center."

That is really specific and demonstrates that you understand what the client has been doing.

That is one example. There are several more.

- Hi Dennis, I'm a major fan of what you're doing at x.ai; we use it internally all the time.
- Hi Dennis, I stumbled across your comments on Google Duplex and found them interesting – I particularly like your approach to company disclosure.
- Hello, Dennis. I've been following your career since Visual Revenue, and I'm quite impressed with what you've developed at x.ai.

- Hi, Dennis. I've been following your tale for a while and finally checked out your LinkedIn; I'm impressed that you have a patent.
- Hey Dennis, I adore the quote on your LinkedIn about Bjorn — it's remarkable how you've infused irreverence across your entire brand.
- Hey Marcy, hello from a fellow UC graduate!
- Hi Marcy, I've been following WPromote for a long time and am impressed with your history... It's wonderful that you progressed from sales associate to head of marketing!
- Hey Marcy, I appreciate what you're doing at WPromote, especially your work with Pied Piper.
- Hi Marcy, I'm a great Zenni fan, so I had to reach out when I noticed you run their campaigns!
- Hi Marcy, I really like your work with Weinerschnitzel.
- Hi Hayley, I adore everything about Golden Hippo and am pleased with your IT background.
- Hey, Hayley, I found you on LinkedIn and adore what you're doing — it's fantastic that you emphasize the importance of critical listening; I believe the same thing.
- Hi Hayley, I came across Golden Hippo and liked the remark from Alyssa on your website; it's impressive how well you treat the QA crew.
- Hi Hayley, I saw you were recruiting a business analyst and wanted to say congratulations on your success!
- Hello, Hayley. I've been following the Golden Hippo Instagram for a while and appreciate how you handle the IT team.

Okay, now you have a general concept. That was an excessive number of compliments, but you now have an example of almost every form of compliment you may write.

You can compliment the receiver on corporate news, department news, their career, revenue, stock price, or anything else that has been reported recently. Just do not go too far. A well-written first line will include just enough information to show that you've personalized it, but not so much that you come across as a stalker! Keep that in mind: shorter is better. One sentence is sufficient.

I'd also like to add something very crucial at this time. Numerous AI technologies out there claim to write personalized first lines. They are always improving, and I see a future in which they will replace humans, but they are not yet ready as of the publication date.

Right now, it's preferable to write them yourself. Once you've completed 100, you can hire a custom first-line writer through Upwork. But I always recommend performing the work yourself before hiring someone else to do it. So, your job for this portion is to write 100 custom first lines, one for each lead you generated in the previous chapter.

Case Study

The next step is to do a case study. An excellent example is the million-dollar email that we deployed at X27, which helped generate $600,000 in yearly recurring revenue in just 60 days, followed by millions.

Here's the case study from that email:

I specialize in bringing new clients to web and app developers. Recently, we assisted Dom & Tom, a NYC-based developer, in bringing on McDonald's and closing an additional $1 million in six months.

Below are some potential examples:

We recently helped Marvel Studios get 250,000 Twitter followers in two weeks using targeted Twitter marketing. We helped Palantir close $500,000 in new contracts in six months by leveraging our brand guidelines and logo to boost their value.

Another example: Our AI-powered suggestions saved LinkedIn $7 million on DevOps recruits in only 60 days.

So we need to write something similar for your organization. Here's something to remember:

A case study is about more than simply numbers. Every word in the case study is purposefully written. And every phrase in the case study is crucial. It is about exhibiting experience, rapidly establishing authority, and eliciting the desired response from the recipient.

Interestingly, the widespread belief that people must know and like you to buy from you is incorrect! This is absolutely incorrect. People don't have to like you; they just need to trust you and know you'll deliver. Microsoft, for example, is a widely despised firm that sells Windows worldwide despite it being a highly despised product! In outrageous amounts!

Call to Action

The next phase in the process is a call to action. This is the easiest ingredient because it is almost always the same.

Before we continue, remember that the purpose of your cold email is to set up a meeting. This is why each email concludes with a "yes" or "no" question. "Mind if I send over a few times for a quick call?" is one example. It must be simple to accept or decline because the people you're prospecting are busy. They don't have time to screw around! Your purpose isn't to encourage people to click on your portfolio, view a wacky, personalized video, or subscribe to your email list. It's simply to get them to meet so that you can close on a five or six-figure transaction. Every other use of cold email wastes this wonderful instrument.

Another crucial part of the call to action is that it is meaningful. You want to schedule a meeting, so don't waste time discussing or requesting things that aren't vital. Don't ask for newsletter signups or other such minor requests! Request meetings that lead directly to sales. Because your time is valuable, as is the recipient's, and you don't want to squander it on meaningless tasks. Similarly, as previously stated, you must go in with large box things. It's futile to sell a $200 product via cold email. If you're unsure about what you're offering, add zero to the price, and you'll thank me later!

The first example of an effective call to action is the "simple ask": "Interested? Let me know, and I'll send over a few times to chat."

The other we call the 'specific benefit.' This one is a bit more advanced: "Can you take on additional clients? Let me know. And I can send you a couple of messages to chat."

The second one is more complex because the initial few words are tailored to your specific offer, rather than copying and pasting the same text as everyone else.

Dealing with the Process

Now, I see that this chapter is especially thorough, with some really specific instances. I also understand that the process involved is not always motivating or appealing. I'm also aware that you may not want to do this. You may believe it is a time-consuming process you are unwilling to do.

That is okay. You are not required to accomplish anything you do not wish to do in this life. Nobody is pushing you to do this. But I'd want to emphasize the importance of this procedure.

What you do with this vital information is entirely up to you. You are under no obligation to use it in any way. However, if you do not apply the lessons we have presented here, you will miss out on a tremendous opportunity. And I believe that no successful firm can afford to overlook this opportunity.

Don't let any obstacles prevent you from mastering cold email. Don't listen to that nagging voice that constantly tells you to be lazy to win! Please put in the effort required to master cold email because it is the most efficient way to schedule meetings, especially in your company's five to six-figure area.

SEND YOUR COLD EMAIL

Y ou've just discovered the secret of cold email. You know how it works and how it will affect your business. You're almost ready to hit 'Send.' However, several questions must be addressed first.

How Many Emails?

First things first, how many emails will you send? Are you planning to shoot thousands of rounds every day? Or do you only glance at one email every day? That is the first question that we will address in this part.

When approaching cold email for the first time, remember that slow and steady wins the race. Hare and Tortoise. You will not grow swiftly; you will gradually gather momentum over time. It's natural to want to jump into the deep end. However, if you start too aggressively with cold email advertising, you may immediately run into a few problems.

First, your campaign is not properly optimized. You might send 1,000 emails and discover that the open rate is barely 17%. This would naturally signal that something is wrong with the system. You might assume, "Okay, we'll fix it," but it's not that simple. You've now burned leads, put yourself at risk of being flagged as spam, and (worst of all) sent a campaign that could have done eight times better with a few modifications.

However, if you are more patient, you can eventually send 1,000 emails daily or more, resulting in a considerably higher open rate, booking far more meetings, and closing far more deals. If you start small, there's no reason you can't increase your open rate to 80% and your meeting booking rate to 6% or higher.

It's also worth noting that when it comes to scaling up, you may not want to by the time you can send 1,000 emails. If you schedule 6 meetings for every 100 emails, 1,000 emails a day equates to 60 meetings per day, which will necessitate a slew of new employment for most small firms. That is why you want to get to the point where your cold email campaigns are so effective and predictable that you can select the number of emails to send to achieve the desired result. So you understand that you can be successful with a modest number of emails. Less work for better results makes sense, right?

However, to reach that stage, things must be properly optimized. First, I'd recommend that you reread the email warming part. This isn't an optional addition; it's necessary. You must warm up your email inbox for at least two weeks before sending; otherwise, you will be flagged as spam and will have to start over.

Now, let's talk about scaling emails. During the first week, send ten cold emails each day. You can then increase it by 10 emails per day for the first month until you send out 100 tailored emails daily. Throughout this process, you should keep track of the overall number of emails sent, including follow-ups. This allows you to avoid exceeding any maximum email limits set by Gmail or Outlook.

Just keep things steady for a time so you can thoroughly test the method and maintain your domain. After the first month, you may monitor your spam score with online tools, and if there are any red lights or noticeably higher spam rates, you can pause the process. If everything is going according to plan, you can start increasing the numbers.

Many people are unaware that Gmail has a daily email limit. If you sign up for the trial account, you can send out 2,000 emails every day at the time of writing. Remember that if you send 1,000 cold emails daily and follow up on many of them, you'll rapidly reach the 2,000 mark. So, before you go anywhere near this figure, ensure your campaigns are running properly.

Another crucial aspect is to ensure that every email you send is aimed at an email address that could potentially result in a purchase.

This is not a "spray and pray" strategy! We are using a targeted and tailored cold email technique. Before sending an email, research each prospect on your lead list. Look at their website to see whether they're a good fit for your service and whether they are the appropriate size of firm to target. This is also an excellent chance to compose your personalized first line. Do your study, stick to your sending restrictions, and you'll be able to start building momentum.

Do not scale your campaign unless you are meeting the benchmarks. If you aren't meeting your goals, your method can be improved; start small before expanding your business. Otherwise, you're wasting leads and money.

What Is the Best Time to Send

Another common question from coaching clients is when is the optimum time to send emails. The first thing to consider when addressing this is how people conduct their professional lives. People prefer to read their work emails at specific times throughout the day and week. So, the optimal times to send emails are first thing in the morning and at the end of the working day because these are the times when most people check their email inboxes.

It is also crucial to consider time zones. Ensure you know where the individual you're sending an email is and that your approach is tailored to that area. Don't simply think about countries; keep in mind that the United States is divided into multiple time zones. 10 am in Philadelphia does not equal 10 am in San Francisco.

Different times of day are also more suitable for different job titles and roles. CEOs, for example, are more likely to check their emails first thing in the morning and late at night, especially if they work for fast-growing firms. It's also better to send on Tuesdays or Wednesdays, as mailing right before the weekend or first thing Monday morning doesn't work well. People don't care about emails before the weekend! They had too much to do on Monday morning. Another option is to send it on Sunday afternoon since many people will be preparing their week ahead of time, making this a good opportunity to target busy people in particular.

Sending Your First Campaign

Okay, let's prepare to send your first campaign. You've performed your exercises and homework, written your cold email, and know what you're selling and who will buy it. So, let's send some emails!

Again, cold email can be really effective; you can accomplish unbelievable results. However, it can also go horribly wrong, resulting in campaigns that go nowhere! But most importantly, the entire procedure is a learning curve. You are one step closer to success as long as you are learning.

Let me give you an example of a terrible marketing. Imagine launching a firm based on a database of SaaS solutions. This allows consumers to rank them and find the best tool recommendations for their needs. So, going ahead to compile a list of firms that may require SaaS services, with an email that reads something like this:

Hello,

I'm researching launching a new SaaS firm and would like to know what challenges you've encountered using SaaS products.

What's the major issue with this email? It does not schedule a meeting or target sales. So, all we got were half-hearted responses. However, this was the suggested cold email tactic at the time! If I were writing the email today, I would probably try the following:

Hey, John.

I created a platform that provides the best SaaS choices for your company.

It starts at $5 a month and includes ten recommendations to reboot all of the tools you're currently using, allowing you to save more money and accomplish more.

Interested?

And from there, you can determine whether someone will buy. That is the distinction between when we tried and failed and what we do now. However, it's all a learning curve. You won't get everything right the first, second, or even fifth time! But if you keep grinding away, learning, and growing, there is a lot you can accomplish with cold email.

Appointment Setting

Sending an effective cold email is no longer enough. You must also communicate with the clients to schedule a meeting, known as 'appointment scheduling.' So, how do you do it? First and foremost, remember that we are doing this to set up a meeting. We're not selling by email; we'd want to receive a phone call to chat with the client directly.

As a result, every response to your cold email should be geared toward this phone conversation, during which you'll close the sale.

So, let me give you some scripts that we've used to schedule these sessions.

Hi, Mike.

Sure thing. I'm available Thursday and Friday from 12 to 1 pm PST next week. Would either of these work for you?

Thanks,

John Doe

If you don't hear back from them, you can continue to follow up. There are several approaches to dealing with this, but one of my favorite responses is simply:

I am bumping this up!

While we're on the subject, your initial client encounter should last only 15-30 minutes. You're just testing the waters to see if they'll be a good fit for you and, more critically, if they can afford your services.

Here's another example.

Hello, Jeffrey.

Would Tuesday at 1:30 or 2 pm PST work?

Let me know, and I'll send you a calendar invite.

Thanks,

John Doe

It is critical always to provide exact times for meetings since it makes it easy for the customer to schedule and saves unnecessary back and forth. I've discovered that busy people love it when you take the initiative, so don't feel the need to slink around. Another suggestion is that while calendar booking tools are accessible, many high-level executives are over 50 and struggle with current technologies. In my experience, offering time slots works better than calendar invites.

Here's another example.

Hi, Jeffrey.

What about next week?

Any day between 11:30 am and 12:30 pm or 5:30 pm and 6:30 pm PST would be ideal from my perspective.

Please let me know if any of these times work for you.

Regards,

John Doe

Another crucial consideration is the optimal time to schedule the meetings. Booking meetings during your clients' working days will yield the best results. If you're on UK time and your clients are in the United States, be prepared to transmit sessions in the early morning and late evening.

So that's how you go about scheduling the meeting. However, not everything will always go according to plan. We must expect the unexpected! What happens if someone fails to show up? Let's go through the steps to avoid this as much as possible.

Benchmarking and Improving Your Campaign

It's vital to emphasize what you should be aiming for. Your open rate should be 80%, your response rate should be at least 15%, and your meeting booking rate should range from 4% to 8%. The subject line and lead quality will be the most critical aspects in meeting these standards, so start there if you don't meet your targets.

But how else can you optimize your marketing to increase your results?

The first thing to remember is that you cannot expect to achieve significant success right away. Anything worthwhile takes patience, and this notion certainly applies to cold email. As previously stated, you must start small and gradually expand. You won't get everything perfect right away. If you expect this to be a quick silver bullet in which you send 50 emails and your calendar is completely packed, you'll be extremely disappointed. That is simply not realistic. You will only get out of this what you put into it, and cold emailing demands three Ts in addition to the three Cs: time, training, and tenacity.

If you are unwilling to put in the initial effort, you will not achieve the desired results, which will be a disappointment. So, you must be patient, fully invested in the process, and willing to tweak and re-tweak every aspect of your cold email strategy. However, if you approach the table with the appropriate attitude, you can accomplish a great deal with the strategy detailed in this book. It may take six months, but you will succeed if you are completely devoted to the process.

That being said, one of the most essential factors in improving cold email outcomes is lead quality. Ensure that you only send emails to customers who are likely to buy from you. Prospects will only respond if they understand what you're selling, so a low response rate indicates that either your email fails to convey your message succinctly, recipients perceive it as spam, or your offer is completely irrelevant to your target market. So, make sure your one-sentence case study is as clear as possible. Make your emails brief and concise, and ensure they are very clear.

If you run into problems, show the email you're sending to a buddy. Have them read it and then tell you what you're selling. If they are unable to do so, your email will need to be rewritten to be simpler and more direct. This issue can generate a lot of problems, especially in the technology area, where the disparities and use cases between different organizations can be tough to discuss objectively. If you're selling a tech product or service, this is definitely something you should focus on.

The response rate is the primary metric. If you are receiving responses, you are well on your path to success. However, if you have a high response rate but are unable to book appointments, you should reassess your follow-up strategy and appointment setup approach. Remember to aim for at least 6 meetings for every 100 emails sent.

The simplest strategy to schedule more meetings is to shorten the delay between their response and your follow-up. So, if someone expresses interest, respond within 5 minutes and watch your meeting booking rate skyrocket.

People who are busy and important do not want to waste time. You need to convince them that you are incredibly valuable to them quickly. Otherwise, they will forget about you, get rid of you, and move on to something else, never giving you another consideration.

Another major concern is the bounce rate. You must keep this under 8% at all times. Make sure your emails are verified before sending them, and keep an eye on the quality of your email leads. If you are seeing irregular bounce rates, it is time to choose a new lead database. Nothing is worse than putting in work only to find out that it was utterly squandered; thus, you must stay on top of this situation.

Testing Plan

It's also crucial to test your cold email technique consistently. Keep trying new things to observe how they affect the whole process and your results.

Here are some options.

- For every 100 emails you send, use 50% with one subject line and 50% with another.
- Test different case studies and language.
- Adjust the sending times for different days and hours.
- Try alternative wording and techniques when sending follow-up emails.

Remove everything that is ineffective from each of these tactics, then conduct more testing with alternative proportions and combinations. The choice is yours, but you should not send cold emails without first measuring the process and experimenting with new ways regularly.

Increasing Cold Email Results

Here are some more things you can do to improve your performance. Everything is now in place for you to implement your cold email plan. However, I'd like to discuss some advanced methods for taking your cold email campaigns to the next level. You may do additional softer things to improve your outcomes beyond the standard degree of optimization.

Building trust is the most effective way to convince prospects to respond. You want your clients to believe you are an expert, that you are a trustworthy person to work with, and that their investment of time and money is safe and prudent. So, if you want to passionately improve your cold email outcomes, you must proportionally boost the client's trust.

But how can you develop trust?! The first approach is to present a compelling and highly relevant case study that speaks directly to the recipients. The stronger the case study, the more relevant it is to the industry you're targeting, and the more it speaks to the person you're contacting, the more trust you'll get. The ideal example would be a case study involving collaboration with a competitor, as this provides social proof of something in common with the target. That equates to instant trust building, which is money in the bank.

The second option is a no-brainer proposition. If you want a client to trust you, your no-brainer offer should involve no consideration at all. So, if you want to strike gold with a cold email, ensure your offer is relevant to your target market. So that someone reads it and immediately decides to buy from you.

The third and last strategy to improve your cold email success is to create a personal brand that shows that you are an authority in your subject. This can be accomplished through social media accounts, YouTube, podcasts, blogs, or a dynamic website presence. It's anything that shows folks you're an authority in your field. Having links online to back up your claims in your cold email will significantly improve your results.

So, if you constantly follow everything we've done thus far, you'll have the ideal cold email and a profitable campaign. That is the ultimate goal. It will not happen right away, so if you don't succeed the first time, keep trying, testing, and improving. Because if you persist with it, you will eventually achieve success.

Everyone who has gotten this to work is shocked! They feel like they've discovered a superpower! They can profit from anybody and everything at any time. So make sure you persevere through the difficult times. Clients will tell you they are uninterested, people will urge you to stop cold emailing, and even your friends and family will warn you that it is a bad idea! But if you persevere, you will reach the other side and achieve tremendously. It simply depends on how much you want it.

UNLOCKING YOUR TEAM'S POTENTIAL FOR LONG-TERM SUCCESS

In this chapter, we'll look into essential mindset traits and practical steps to significantly enhance your effectiveness as a leader. Embracing the right mindset is vital, whether you're aiming to improve your team dynamics, drive your business forward, or advance your career.

It's important to shift your perspective from merely viewing your work as a means to generate income. While financial success is certainly important, the true value of your efforts lies in your ability to make a positive, lasting impact. Let's look at how you can cultivate a purpose-driven mindset and implement actionable strategies that can transform your approach to leadership even as you work with cold emails.

Four Critical Obligations

No matter the size or nature of your organization, you're constantly learning and discovering new insights on the job. However, some broad principles remain universally effective, regardless of your position. Whether you're a junior manager just starting out or the CEO of a large corporation, these principles are timeless and consistently deliver results. Your status within the company doesn't change its relevance; it applies to everyone in a leadership role.

Obligation to Your Employees

Your first and foremost obligation is to the people who work with you. As a leader, it's essential to ensure that your team members are happy and fulfilled and feel they are on a positive career trajectory. You might think this requires taking bold or disruptive actions, but no. The best way to meet this obligation is to cultivate a culture of openness and flexibility, where you avoid making assumptions about anyone and instead empower them to carve their own path.

Let's imagine a scenario involving a team member named Jack. Jack works in our marketing department, where he's responsible for managing client relationships and generating leads. However, outside of work, Alex has a deep passion for videography and runs a successful YouTube channel. On this channel, he shares content related to digital marketing strategies, some of which touch upon techniques we use within our company.

One day, I came across Jack's channel during a routine check of our social media mentions. He had posted several videos discussing our strategies, explaining them in an engaging and informative way. My first reaction was one of concern. In many large corporations, this kind of independent content creation could be seen as a potential conflict of interest, especially if it involves company-specific practices. There could have been immediate questions about confidentiality, brand representation, and the line between personal and professional identities.

It would have been easy for us to take a defensive stance. We could have asked Jack to take down the videos or, worse, initiated disciplinary action, fearing that his content might somehow jeopardize our brand or reveal too much of our internal strategies. However, instead of jumping to conclusions, I decided to have a conversation with him.

When I sat down with Jack, I was genuinely curious to understand his motivations. He explained that his passion for digital marketing extended beyond his work at our company. He found joy in creating content that could help others improve their marketing skills. The videos he posted were a reflection of this passion and his respect for the work we do. In fact, his content was inspired by the training and resources we provide internally. He wasn't trying to expose or undermine our processes; he was simply enthusiastic about sharing knowledge and helping others grow.

Hearing this, I realized that Jack's intentions were aligned with the values we uphold as a company. Rather than stifling his creativity, I saw an opportunity to harness it. I proposed that we support his content creation by providing him access to a video editor and offering him a share of the sponsorship revenue generated by our main YouTube channel. This way, not only could he continue pursuing his passion, but he could also bring greater visibility to our company's expertise.

This decision had a profound impact. Jack was thrilled by the support and felt more connected to our organization than ever before. His enthusiasm spilled over into his work, and he became even more dedicated to his role in the marketing department. By supporting Jack, we also gained a new avenue for showcasing our brand authentically and engagingly. His channel began attracting a wider audience, many of whom became interested in our services.

This experience reinforced a crucial lesson: as leaders, our role is to manage and empower. By recognizing and nurturing our team members' unique talents and passions, we can foster a culture of innovation and loyalty. It's a simple yet powerful approach that many companies, particularly large ones, often overlook. Unlike tech giants such as Apple, Google, and Meta, smaller businesses can't afford to stifle potential innovators. Instead, we should aim to enable them, as their success is intrinsically linked to our own.

By allowing your employees to express themselves and be who they want to be, you will unlock levels of motivation and productivity that you never imagined.

Your team will be happier, and ultimately, wouldn't you prefer to lead an organization filled with happy, engaged people rather than disappointed ones?

Obligation to Your Customers

Equally important to your employees is your obligation to your customers. It's crucial to ensure that your customers have confidence in what you're doing. They need to be assured that what you're selling is not a scam and that you consistently deliver on your promises—from the functionality of your product to customer service and refunds.

This obligation extends to every level of your organization. For example, I occasionally make calls to my sales team to see how quickly they answer the phone. This isn't about micromanaging; it's about ensuring that everything is running smoothly and understanding the customer's experience firsthand. Your business exists in the mind of the customer, so if they have a bad experience, they'll perceive your company as bad, regardless of your internal opinion. It's crucial to stay connected with your customers' perspectives, even if you believe you're doing an excellent job. What matters is whether your customers agree with that assessment.

Obligation to Yourself

Lastly, you have an obligation to yourself. It's vital to ensure that you are excited about running your business. Your performance will naturally improve when you're genuinely passionate about your work. However, this obligation also includes creating an environment where your team is equally motivated to tackle their tasks, ensuring their work is valuable and ethically sound.

There will be times when you encounter tasks that feel mundane and uninspiring. However, a small shift in perspective can often transform even the most tedious tasks into something more engaging. Imagine, for instance, a scenario with Emily, a marketing director at a growing tech startup.

Emily is responsible for creating content for her company's educational platform. Typically, she enjoys the creative process, but after months of producing similar content, she began to feel burned out. One day, her team requested that she produce a series of tutorial videos based on the company's existing training materials. The thought of rehashing old content felt like a drag, and Emily found herself dreading the task. She even considered postponing it to favor something more exciting, but she knew the project was important for onboarding new clients.

As Emily sat down to brainstorm, she realized that her lack of enthusiasm stemmed from the repetitiveness of the task. She knew she needed to approach it differently to get through it. After some reflection, she decided to focus on making the project as efficient as possible while still adding value. Instead of re-recording all the material, she chose to film only each video's closing segments. This allowed her to condense the content into shorter, more digestible clips, which would serve as a quick refresher for clients already familiar with the basics.

This small adjustment made the task more manageable and reignited her interest in the project. By shifting her focus and finding a new angle, Emily was able to complete the entire series in a single afternoon. What initially seemed like a daunting, uninspiring task turned into a productive session that left her feeling accomplished.

The key takeaway here is that you can find excitement in your job, even in the more tedious tasks, by simply tweaking your approach. As a manager, it's your responsibility to ensure that you're enthusiastic about your work. How can you expect your team to feel the drive if you're not motivated and don't believe in what you're doing?

Obligation to the Business

One of the most critical responsibilities of a manager is to the business itself. Simply put, if your business isn't thriving, neither will you. This responsibility operates on multiple levels, but I want to particularly highlight the importance of fostering a positive culture. Whether you're working for a corporation or running it, engaging in morally questionable practices will ultimately hinder your success. Even if you achieve financial success, it won't feel fulfilling. That's why it's strongly recommended that everyone, regardless of their position in the company, act as if they own the business. They should care about the company's reputation as if it were their own.

When I first joined an advertising firm in Chicago, I was just starting out as a junior sales representative alongside a colleague I'll refer to as Daniel Foster. We were both new to the industry, learning the ropes and trying to make our mark in a competitive environment.

The early days were challenging. Daniel and I spent countless hours cold-calling potential clients, attending networking events, and refining our sales pitches. We were eager to prove ourselves, but the work was often grueling, with little immediate reward. Despite this, I found myself increasingly drawn to the strategic aspects of the business. I started noticing areas where our firm could improve—ways to streamline our processes, enhance client relationships, and ultimately, grow the business.

Imagine starting your career at a marketing firm in New York as a junior sales associate alongside a colleague named John. Years later, you've risen to the position of marketing director and even started your own successful business, with that same New York firm now as one of your loyal clients. Meanwhile, John is still in his junior sales role. The key difference? You decided to take control of your situation, realizing that you wanted to be your own boss. With that clarity, you dedicated yourself to making the organization more efficient, leading to the company's best performance within a few months.

As a manager, you hold significant power. You can build a successful business. The responsibility stops with you. If the business fails or underperforms, it's on you. So always do everything you can to ensure that your business is effective, productive, and has an exciting, rewarding culture.

If you're working for a company and get fired for trying to make it better, see it as a blessing in disguise. It's an opportunity to find a company that truly values you and what you bring to the table. If your boss fires you for striving to improve the organization, the consequences are on both of you.

Driving Alignment with Cold Email

How can you successfully sell the cold email process within your organization? There are 2 powerful approaches to enhance your sales team's effectiveness.

First, focus on mission alignment. Ensure that every sales team member understands the "why" behind their roles. If someone is solely motivated by the paycheck, they may not be the right fit. Everyone must grasp the broader purpose of what you're doing. This understanding can make a world of difference.

Consider two sales representatives with the chance to close a $250,000 deal. The first rep is fixated on their $25,000 commission, while the second rep recognizes not just the financial gain but also how the product will transform the client's organization and impact the lives of its customers. The second rep, who sees the true value of what they're selling, is far more likely to close the deal because their approach resonates beyond just the monetary aspect.

The second strategy is to introduce a healthy dose of competition among your salespeople. For example, if Jack books 8 meetings, that's great—but if Jennifer books 25, Jack now has a new benchmark. This context motivates him to improve and creates an environment where team members can evaluate their performance, learn from each other, and share best practices.

Proactive Compensation

Most people understand what they want. They only need permission to ask for it. But most CEOs do the following:

Hey, gentlemen, we've started a new effort in which we'll send 1,000 cold emails per week. Please let me know when that is finished. I need 1,000 emails sent out before the end of the week as soon as possible.

That is one way to approach it. Here's another approach.

Hey, gentlemen, we have a new effort to send cold emails since it will greatly improve the organization, and we will schedule many meetings. How many emails do you believe are feasible to send in a week?

You may receive various responses by asking employees what they believe is reasonable. They might say twenty! But then you may have a conversation with them and involve them in the decision-making process. "Most teams deliver 1,000. "You think you can only do twenty?" They immediately get more ownership.

This applies to compensation as well. Consider asking employees what they believe is reasonable remuneration based on the budget rather than simply telling them their salary. Again, this relates to the overall concept of making people feel valued, empowering them, and constantly engaging them with the organization.

You're not simply treating them like workhorses who will grind themselves to dust for the company; you're actually including them in the process. They are stakeholders.

And your salesperson will likely request a smaller commission than you were willing to pay. It may be a win-win scenario. The crucial thing is that merely participating in the debate makes your employees feel valued, which is exactly the opposite approach to my conversation in New York that led to my becoming an entrepreneur. You do not want that. You do not want your greatest folks to leave to do their own thing. You want them to continue working for you indefinitely.

So, if you've learned anything from this chapter, it's that people will do whatever they want, whether you're present or not. As a result, your duty as a manager is to identify the individuals who will thrive in your firm and foster an environment that will allow them to achieve.

As a manager, it is not your responsibility to alter people or force them to do things they do not want to do or, more importantly, do not believe in. You are in the talent identification and hype business! And if you can find the appropriate people and enthuse them about working for you, the sky is the limit!

CONCLUSION

You now have everything that you could possibly need. You have no excuse. You can start using cold email today and achieve untold success and wealth. You are the only thing standing in your way of success. It would be best if you were invested in the process.

This is the simplest, quickest, and most effective technique to increase clientele for your firm. You do not need any other information. No other podcasts, channels, or courses will contribute anything to what you've read here. All of the information and knowledge is at your fingertips.

There are no more excuses. We've paved the way for your success. It would be best not to look back in a few years and regret not taking action. The solution to your issues is here, and it's up to you to use it. You're ready for success, and it's within your reach.

Don't underestimate the power and potential of what you hold in your hands. Cold email is the key to resolving any income issues you've ever encountered in your organization. A few emails could change everything. You have nothing to lose and everything to gain. Seize the opportunity. Now!

.

www.ingramcontent.com/pod-product-compliance
Lightning Source LLC
Chambersburg PA
CBHW071502210326
41597CB00018B/2662